The Role of Tourism in Poverty Alleviation in Tanzania

The Role of Tourism in Poverty Alleviation in Tanzania

Research Report No. 03.4

Nathanael Luvanga
Joseph Shitundu
(University of Dar es Salaam)

RESEARCH ON POVERTY ALLEVIATION

MKUKI NA NYOTA PUBLISHERS LTD
P. O. BOX 4246, DAR ES SALAAM, TANZANIA

Published for: Research on Poverty Alleviation (REPOA)
P. O. Box 33223, Dar es Salaam, Tanzania
www.repoa.or.tz

By: Mkuki na Nyota Publishers
P. O. Box 4246, Dar es Salaam, Tanzania
www.mkukinanyota.com

ISBN 9987-686-65-6

Table of Contents

LIST OF TABLES

LIST OF FIGURES

ABBREVIATIONS

DFID	Department for International Development
Dpt	Department
EIA	Environment Impact Assessment
GDP	Gross Domestic Product
GNP	Gross National Product
Kms	Kilometres
NGOs	Non Governmental Organisations
ODI	Overseas Development Institute
REPOA	Research on Poverty Alleviation
TIC	Tanzania Investment Centre
Tshs	Tanzanian Shillings
UNESCO	United Nations Education, Science and Cultural Organisation
US $	United States Dollar
USA	United States of America
WTO	World Tourism Organisation

ABSTRACT

Poverty alleviation is currently a major concern for many developing countries including Tanzania. Higher economic growth rate that is pro-poor is a pre-requisite in the process of poverty alleviation. During the last one and half decades of socio-economic reforms in Tanzania, rapid growth rate in the tourism sector has been recorded in terms of tourist arrivals, tourism activities (services) and earnings.

With its distinct advantages tourism is postulated as another important industry for poverty alleviation. The advantages include among others, creation of job opportunities; boosting up of sales of different goods and services such as agricultural products and handcrafts, as well as cultural entertainment performed by locals the majority of whom are poor. The industry is also an important in-let for the much needed foreign exchange. As such tourism as an industry can play very important roles on economic, improved livelihoods and socio-cultural development that are critical for poverty alleviation.

However, tourism is a complex industry, which is driven by the private sector and often by large international companies, which may have little or no interest in ensuring that poverty is alleviated among the locals. It is also possible that with the current technological development that tourism earnings remain outside the destination country due to leakages. In addition, tourism can cause negative impacts such as environmental problems, cultural pollution and immoral behaviour including that of prostitution.

The concern of the study is that while earnings from tourism may look impressive, one would like to know more about its impact on the livelihoods of the locals before concluding that this is a positive development that should be promoted. This is particularly, because, as with all modernization efforts leading to economic growth, there are costs and benefits implications.

Thus, as Tanzania is rapidly becoming a major tourist destination, it is worthwhile to examine the effects of this industry on poverty alleviation through the enhancement of the nation's economy and the improved livelihoods of the people in tourist areas.

1.0 INTRODUCTION

1.1 BACKGROUND

Poverty alleviation is of a major concern for many developing countries including Tanzania. Poverty can be alleviated mainly through achieving higher sectoral growth and ensuring that the poor have a share in that growth. There is evidence that tourism contributes a lot to the economic growth of even countries with poor economies through foreign exchange earnings, creation of employment opportunities and provision of public revenues.[1] With proper interventions, such economic benefits can play a crucial role in the process of poverty alleviation. In general, tourism has become a significant industry in both poor and rich economies because of its important impacts on economic, livelihoods and socio-cultural development (Shah 2000).

This study shows that apart from economic impacts, tourism affects the livelihood of the poor and that, if properly harnessed the positive impacts from the sector can contribute towards poverty alleviation.

1.2 STATEMENT AND SIGNIFICANCE OF THE PROBLEM

1.2.1 Statement of the Problem

Earnings from tourism look impressive, but one would like to know more about its economic implications before concluding that this is a positive development that should be promoted. One would like to know the net (national) benefits from tourism, deducting extra cost from gross revenues, and also who benefits from these net earnings. And whether such economic earnings have anything to do with poverty alleviation.

As with all modernisation efforts leading to economic growth, there are costs and benefits implications as well. These may be important, as tourism is a peculiar export of services, with no actual services leaving the country but with its clients coming to enjoy these inside the exporting nation. Therefore, at a time when Tanzania is rapidly becoming a major tourist destination, getting ready for the quantum leap towards mass tourism, it seems worthwhile to examine its effects to the economy in general and the poor in particular.

---

[1] See Sinclair (1998).

1

1.2.2 Significance of the Problem

The significance of the problem arises from the intended goal of trying to quantify the economic effects of tourism in Tanzania and their contribution towards poverty alleviation. In so doing, the study sheds light on what the government can do to maximise economic benefits and minimise costs. This is in line with the governmentís objective of trying to ensure that the tourism industry is elevated to a giant contributor to the national economy by not just realising high income figures but also making sure that the host country benefits.

This corroborates the Presidentís speech, His Excellency Benjamin William Mkapa, as follows, ìT otal figures on tourism show the income and outlay of the tourists themselves, omitting any currency outflow or financial transfers related to investments and the presence of foreigners in the sectorÖ. Investors and tour operators have to get a decent return on their investment and operations but all stake holders including the host country must also benefit substantially.î [2]

The study is also significant due to its endeavour to identify and suggest ways in which tourism can be used to contribute towards poverty alleviation. Beginning 1993 the Government of Tanzania (GoT) has been (through reforms) attracting private investment in most sectors including the tourism sector where private investments have shown some success. This study also is an attempt to analyse how a growing sector like tourism can be utilised for poverty alleviation.

1.3 RESEARCH OBJECTIVES AND QUESTIONS

1.3.1 Research Objectives

Broad Objectives

The main objective of the study was to analyse the direct and indirect livelihood impacts from tourism and their implications on poverty alleviation. Being the fastest growing sector in the economy, one would like to know more about the net benefits to the society at large, and in particular to the poor.

Specific Objectives

The specific objectives of the study included attempts to:

    (i)   analyse public costs and benefits involved in tourism investment;

---

[2] Speech by President B. W. Mkapa to the African Association of Tour Operators Conference in Arusha on May 19, 1998.

2

(ii)   establish trends in a number of establishments, employment and incomes of various stakeholders as well as public revenues and foreign exchange resulting from tourism in Tanzania;

(iii)   establish through income and employment multipliers, the impact of tourism on poverty alleviation in Tanzania;

(iv)   analyse the linkages between tourism and other sectors of the economy; and

(v)   identify factors, which could help Tanzania to maximise economic gains from tourism and minimise economic losses from it.

1.3.2 Research Questions

The study analysed the economic effects from tourism and their impact on poverty alleviation in Tanzania. Specific research questions to be answered included the following:

(i)   What is the contribution of the tourism sector in Tanzania towards employment, incomes, foreign exchange and public revenue generation?

(ii)   What are the effects of tourism on the incomes of the poor and other local stakeholders?

(iii)   Which group of the poor is likely to benefit more from the economic benefits tourism?

(iv)   What linkages are there between tourism and other sectors of the economy that are critical for poverty alleviation?

(v)   What are the barriers to seizing economic opportunities created by tourism?

1.4 RESEARCH METHODOLOGY, TECHNIQUES AND HYPOTHESES

1.4.1 Research Methodology

Improved understanding of poverty in recent years has highlighted, among others, the following (See also Ashley and Hussein, 2000):

(i)   Well-being is not only about increased income alone but other dimensions of poverty such as food insecurity, social inferiority, social exclusion, lack of physical assets and vulnerability need to be addressed as well.

3

(ii)   Household poverty is determined by many factors, including lack of access to assets, and lack of influence in policy making institutions.

(iii)   Differences in livelihood practices.

The livelihood approach to development and poverty reduction tries to incorporate all these concerns. Under this approach not only the economic benefits from tourism are examined but also their contribution towards the improvement of the livelihood of the people. A simplified version of this approach was used in this study. It is postulated that for poverty reduction, a livelihood encompasses the capabilities, assets (both material and social resources) and activities required for a means of living. When it comes to its impact on poverty alleviation, it means that changes in measurable indicators (such as cash, yield) must be assessed not in their own right, but in terms of their contribution to the improved livelihood. The contribution may be direct (for instance, adding to income, health, food) or indirect (affecting their assets, activities and options). The model is people centered and attempts to assess impact based on people's own perspectives. Specifically, the model articulates the ownership of assets used for certain strategies and activities in order to generate outcomes that contribute towards poverty alleviation. To arrive towards that end, three key themes need to be explored, namely livelihood strategies, livelihood changes due to tourism and differences between stakeholders. A simplified version of the livelihoods framework is presented in Figure 1:

Figure 1: A simplified livelihoods framework

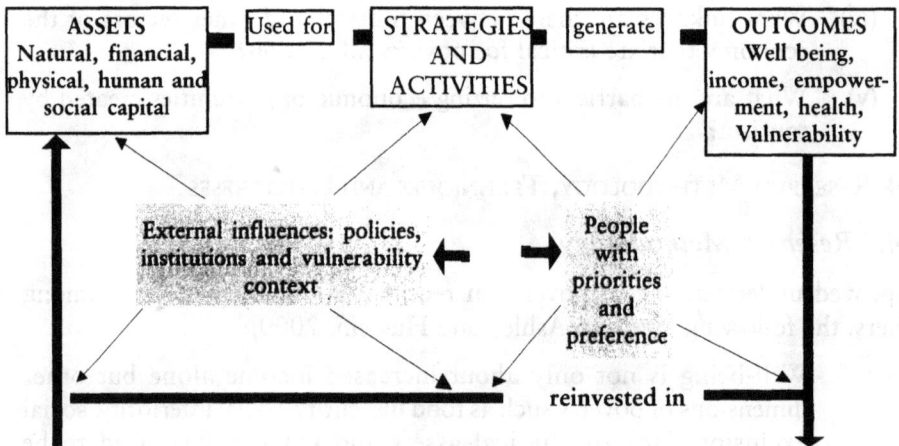

Source: C. Ashley, adapted from DFID (1999) Guidance Sheets and Carney (1998)

4

1.4.2 Study Area

This study covered three areas, one in each of the two regions of Arusha and Coast (Bagamoyo) in Tanzania Mainland and the other in Northern Unguja in Zanzibar (Tanzania Isles). Within the three selected areas, there are significant developments taking place in the tourism sector to warrant analysis of their impact on poverty alleviation. Poverty in Tanzania is basically a rural phenomenon. The three areas apart from being tourist centres have a rural setting as well.

(i)   Arusha region is located in the northern part of Tanzania and it has a wide range of tourist attractions. These include Serengeti National Park, which is undoubtedly the best-known wildlife sanctuary in the world. The Park has a large number of wildebeest and many species of birds. Other attractions include Ngorongoro Crater, Lake Manyara and are almost equally important and famous. The two villages of Mto wa Mbu Barabarani and Kilimamoja have the required characteristics mentioned earlier.

(ii)   Bagamoyo is a famous tourist centre in the Coast Region, situated approximately 65 km north of Dar-es-Salaam along the white sandy beach of the Indian Ocean. It is a place of considerable significance to world history, both as an entry point for Arab and European missionaries, explorers and traders in East and Central Africa in the era of the slave trade. Bagamoyo has considerable charm and presents an opportunity to enjoy old style unspoiled beach holiday combined with visits to the cultural, historical and natural heritage attractions. These include the first church, the Boma, Kaole ruins, the mission museum and many others. The specific areas are Magomeni and Dunda wards.

(iii)   Zanzibar is the world's most famous spicy island. It is in Zanzibar that the African culture blended with other cultures, mainly Persian, Arabic, and Indian and so on to form the Swahili culture. Famous explorers such as Dr. Livingstone, Speke, Burton, Krapt and Rebman launched their exploration to the interior of the African continent from this point. Today the romance, the splendour and legends of the past are still vibrantly alive. These include the traditional sailing dhows, carved wooden doors, chests, and the scent of the clove and the smile of the hospitable residents. All these are great attractions to many tourists who visit the Zanzibar Island. Kiwengwa village in the north-eastern part of the island was specifically studied in Zanzibar.

1.4.3 Sampling Procedure

The methodology adopted for the study distinguishes between local and external stakeholders[3]. Within each location and between participants and non-participants, the central focus of the study was further disaggregated into socio-economic activities and gender participants to the tourism industry. Local participants attributes, as well as the nature and type of involvement were examined. The sampling procedure involved the following steps:

(i)   selecting areas of study within some tourist centres in Arusha, Bagamoyo and Zanzibar.

(ii)   identifying participating and non-participating local stakeholders in each area.

(iii)   100 stakeholders or about 5percent of the estimated population of the area of the study were randomly selected for interview, taking into consideration those living near and far away from the centres (the cut off being a distance of about 5 Kms).

1.4.4 Data Types and Sources

Both secondary and primary data were utilised. To start with, official statistics were collected including a review of earlier studies on tourism in Tanzania.

Secondary information was supplemented with primary data obtained through questionnaire-based interviews. There was need to go beyond secondary data as reliability and method of collection could be questioned, and as some of the important information were not officially available. Therefore, an additional (own) survey in Arusha, Coast region (Bagamoyo) and Zanzibar was implemented to fill in data gaps and possibly correct or improve upon existing data. The survey also provided data used in qualitative analysis.

During the survey, officials in large and small hotels, guesthouses and lodges were questioned in each location, about their trends and their average turnover, occupancy rates, employment, imports and domestic supplies. Other stakeholders such as tour operators, travel agents, service providers (handicrafts, farmers, shop-keepers, vendors, taxi owners, tea stall owners etc.), employees and officials were also interviewed.

---

[3] Stakeholders in this case include all those participating agents such as local community, government institutions, NGOs and individuals.

1.4.5 Data Collection Instruments

The following instruments were used for data collection:

(i)   *Documentation:* This involved collecting information and data from existing reports and documents on tourism.

(ii) *Structured Questionnaires:* This was used so as to generate information and data, which subsequently was used for both qualitative and quantitative analysis. Specific questionnaires for each group were designed.

(iii) *Checklist of Leading Questions:* These questions were designed to guide researchers in conducting dialogue with a range of stakeholders in the tourism sector. The aim was to enable collection of the views of officials in the tourism sector, for instance, on local costs, benefits and tourism policies and plans.

(iv) *Use of informants:* This instrument was used to capture specific changes. Elders and leaders in the areas of study for example, narrated historical information and other changes.

(v)   *Observations:* Observations during the fieldwork was used mainly to assist to probe on issues beyond those which are covered in the structured questionnaire and interview checklist.

1.4.6 Data Analysis

Three levels of analysis were undertaken:

(i)   Descriptive statistics including frequency, tables, percentages and ratios;

(ii) Computation and interpretation of employment and income multipliers;

(iii) Computation and interpretation of linkages between tourism and other sectors such as agriculture.

1.4.7 Hypotheses

The study was guided by the following hypotheses:

(i)   Participation in tourism activities is positively related to poverty reduction through increased employment, incomes and accessibility to livelihood requirements.

(ii)   Participating households near the tourist centres are likely to benefit more than those far away.

(iii)   Households participating in sectors with linkages to tourism are more likely to reduce their poverty from tourism activities than those in sectors with fewer linkages.

2.0 A REVIEW OF THE LINKAGE BETWEEN TOURISM AND POVERTY ALLEVIATION

2.1 THE THEORETICAL LINKAGE BETWEEN TOURISM AND POVERTY

In order to analyse the linkage between tourism and poverty alleviation it is important to define tourism first. The United Nations Conference on International Travel and Tourism of 1963, defined tourists as temporary visitors who spend more than 24 hours in destinations other than their normal place of residence. The motive for the journey should be for holidaymaking, recreation, health, study, religion, sport, visiting family or friends, business or meetings (Sinclair, 1998). The current study adopts this definition. Theoretically, therefore tourism is an economic activity, which belongs to the invisible trade section of the balance of payments accounts. It is deemed to be an export of services to the foreign countries from which the visitors originate. For the local or domestic tourists, tourism is accounted for within the internal trade regime and captured from the relevant sectors.

Given the above, tourism as a sector can theoretically be linked to poverty alleviation by identifying its advantages in the development of local economies.

These include the facts that:

(i)   The consumer (tourist arrivals) comes to the destination, thereby providing opportunities for selling additional goods and services (e.g. agricultural products, handicrafts) produced by locals including the poor. The resulting income and employment generation may help reduce poverty levels particularly income poverty of the local residents including the poor. The fairly poor who participate in these activities may directly reduce their poverty. In addition, the poor can reduce their poverty if the earnings from tourism are used to support their health and education services which are linked to poverty alleviation by improving their well-being and capabilities.

8

(ii)   Tourism is an important opportunity to diversify local economies. It can develop in poor and marginal areas with few other export and diversification options. Remote areas, particularly, attract tourists because of their origin, cultural, wildlife and landscape value. Thus, poverty may be reduced as tourism creates new employment opportunities and income generating activities. Sometimes the infrastructure and social service facilities are established or improved using earnings from tourism. Using such facilities the poor not only improve their incomes but also their social well being and capabilities.

(iii)   Tourism offers labour intensive and small-scale opportunities compared to other non-agricultural activities, it employs a high proportion of women and values natural resources and culture, which may feature among the few assets belonging to the poor. Thus, tourism offers opportunities in terms of employment creation and income generation, to the vulnerable groups such as women to reduce their poverty.

However, there are also (potentially) some negative effects arising from tourism which can have unfavourable economic effects. These include the large-scale transfer of tourism revenue out of the host country and exclusion of local businesses, inhabitants and products. These result into losses of incomes to the displaced particularly because in most cases the tourist industry is highly imports dependent.

In general it is therefore possible that, the poor may gain few direct economic benefits from tourism while bearing many of the costs and hence fail to reduce their poverty. Previous tourism development plans tended to ignore the negative impacts that could be inflicted. In the tourism planning process in most South East Asian countries in the 1970s and the 1980s, for instance, it was assumed that any economic gains tourism brought to local communities would more than compensate any losses. Little attention was given to the impact that diversion of natural resources for tourist facilities would have on local communities or the environment (Shah and Gupta, 2000). Currently, however, most tourism development plans include Environmental Impact Assessments (EIAs) to avoid or minimise the negative impacts (on environment). The idea is find ways of trying to mitigate those costs while maximising the economic benefits to the poor.

Reducing poverty through engaging in tourist activities is theoretically possible. However, due to the process of globalisation, modernisation and information technology the poor may not automatically reduce their poverty through tourism activities. In addition it is also noted that tourism is currently a complex industry, which is driven by the private sector, and often by large international companies, which may have little or no interest in ensuring that poverty is alleviated among the locals.

Leakages also occur, due to use of imported skilled labour and luxury products, repatriation of profits by international companies, and the considerable role of marketing, transport and other services based in the originating country. What is important from a poverty perspective is how much stays in the destination country in general and whether much of it is spent on goods and services of the poor.

2.2 EMPIRICAL REVIEW

Tourism is an important industry in many developing countries providing foreign exchange, employment, incomes and public revenue. It has become an important sector and it potentially constitutes one of the fastest growing sectors. It is one of the top five sources of foreign currency for 83 percent of developing countries. The contribution of tourism receipts to total revenues in these countries is within the range of 80 to 20 percent (Benavides, 2001). During 1980-87, for example, international tourist receipts grew by 45 percent or six times faster than exports in general (Bird, 1992).

In developing countries of Asia, Latin America and Africa, net foreign exchange contribution amounted to 2.6, 2.6 and 0.7 billion dollars respectively in 1986 (Sinclair et al 1995). It is an important foreign exchange earner in many of the Asian economies such as Thailand and Indonesia as well as small-island economies such as Fiji, Jamaica, Bermuda, Maldives and Seychelles (Sinclair, 1998:22). By 1994, tourism provided about 70 percent of total foreign exchange earnings for Seychelles. Tourism became a major foreign exchange earner for Nepal, its share in the total value of merchandise exports more than trebled from 19 per cent in 1973-74 to about 60 percent in 1989 before declining to 36 percent in 1992 (Shah and Gupta, 2000).

Further evidence on the importance of tourism from some African countries indicates that, in Kenya it has overtaken primary commodity exports of coffee and tea accounting for 13 percent of Kenya's exports. By 1988 tourism export earnings reached 37 percent of total Kenya's export earnings relative to 26 percent for coffee and 20 percent for tea (Sinclair et al 1995). In the Gambia, tourism is described as "manna from heaven" which will solve its economic difficulties in terms of contributions to foreign exchange earnings, government revenues, regional development stimuli, and creation of employment (Dieke,

1993:277). It is a second export earner in Gambia and also in Egypt where it follows after remittances from abroad (Gee, 1997). In Tunisia, by mid 1990s, it was the first export earner its revenues covering 60 percent of Tunisia's trade deficit (Focus Multimedia, 1997).

Tourism's contribution to GDP/GNP has been important in a number of countries. In Bali Island (Indonesia), for example, tourism's contribution to GDP is estimated at between 20 to 40 percent. In Nepal the average contribution of tourism earnings to GDP increased from 1percent in 1974 to 4 percent in 1992. During the 1990s its contribution to GDP was 50 percent in Seychelles and to GNP was 32 percent in Barbados, 18 percent in Maldives, 10 percent in Mauritius and 6 percent in Tunisia (Gee, 1997).

Incomes for national citizens related to their employment in the tourist sector are also important. The World Trade Organization (WTO) projects that by the year 2005, tourism jobs will increase faster than those in traditional industries by as much as 59 percent. Employment generation by tourism varies from one economy to another depending on, among others, the size and extent of diversification. For example, in larger and more economically diversified islands, such as Jamaica and Puerto Rico, tourism generates about 5 percent of total employment. In smaller islands the share can go up to one-half and above. For example, in Bermuda tourism employs (direct and indirect) 75 percent of the labour force. In other developing countries the figure is not big, as in Cyprus employment creation lies between 5 percent and 10 percent, in Malta 3.5 percent, in Fiji 5 percent, in Tahiti 3 percent and in Bali less than 1 percent. Direct employment in hotels is the most reliable indicator of the sector's contribution to employment, given that data on other direct employment, indirect employment and capital goods employment is hard to get. In Tunisia and Malta, for example, hotels employ about 0.4 persons per bed. In Bali each twin-bedded room averaged 1.5 employees in 1974, but generally hotel employment affected many more persons since employee turnover averaged twenty-one months.[4] Although larger hotels do better here than small ones, other factors such as location, price category, standard of service do matter.

In Tanzania, official data indicate that there were around 157,000 people supposed to be working in the sector in 2001 compared to 96,000 in 1995 (URT, 2002). This may still be an under-estimation, since indirect employment is not taken into account. In 1996 in Zanzibar, tourism employed directly an estimated 4,000 people and 21,000 indirectly. In Kenya tourism is estimated to

---

[4] See Noranha (1979).

create about 180,000 formal jobs and 380,000 informal ones, a number that could be doubled if tourism was to be managed and planned more properly, with less crime and political violence interrupting the industry.[5] In Tunisia the service sector's (including tourism) contribution to the creation of job opportunities increased from 15 percent of the labour force in 1986 to 36 percent in 1995. In Seychelles the figure rose from 13.5 percent of the labour force in 1985 to 15 percent in 1994 (United States Bureau of Public Affairs 1987, Focus Multimedia, 1997 and Seychelles Home Page). In Malta direct employment in hotels increased from 7,375 employees in 1990 to 9,533 employees in 2000 (Malta Tourism Authority, 2001). In other countries potential and actual job creation may differ widely, but the net balance may still be worthwhile, in view of limited alternatives for job creation. Tourism has the ability to generate employment both in the formal and informal activities. Evidence indicate that the level of employment in tourism activities is high, for example accounting for 0.5 million jobs in Spain and about 5 million in India (Sinclair, 1998).

Employment is also often higher in tourism than in other sectors and wages compare well with other sectors but inversely related to jobs. Wages of hotel employees compare favourably with those in agriculture, and even more when compared to subsistence agriculture. Unskilled hotel employees in Cyprus earned between 50 percent and 75 percent more than other unskilled workers in 1973. Those in managerial positions earned about 25 percent more than those in other sectors. In Tunisia and Spain although industrial workers were earning a bit higher than hotel workers, there was little difference in their living standards (Huit, 1979). More recent information from Nepal indicates that, profits from tourist related activities are higher than those not intended for tourists. For instance, in a 1995 study it was found that profits from fruit cultivation in a district near a National Park were much higher than those from grain crops. Per hectare yields from a fruit orchard was worth ten times that from a paddy field and more than thirty times that from a maize crop. Tourists provided the main market for fruit harvest (Shah and Gupta, 2000). Translated into wages, it is obvious that wages in tourist related activities (fruits) would be higher than those in non-tourist related activities.

Tax revenues to the government, both direct and indirect ones, are also an important benefit from tourism. Unfortunately, even in the most popular tourist destinations little thought has gone into designing the most appropriate level

---

[5] According to a report in the Daily Nation, April 1998.

and form of taxation to be imposed. The impression exists that tax revenues from tourism could be substantially higher than at present, although information on the nature and importance of government revenues from tourism is scanty. Early evidence for sampled countries provides estimates for tax revenue in the order of 20 percent of (gross) tourist receipts. In Tunisia, net budgetary impact (budgetary receipts less budgetary costs on infrastructure, incentives, promotion) came to 15 to 20 percent of receipts. Indirect tax receipts accounted for 10 percent. In Kenya the 1966-67 budgetary receipts were estimated at 28 percent of tourist receipts, budgetary outlays at 8 percent leaving a net return to the budget of 20 percent. World Bank estimates from tourist projects show that budgetary receipts generated by tourist expenditures are in the range of one-fifth and one-third of tourist receipts. In Maldives in 1984, government revenues from tourism accounted for 40 percent. However, the level of tax exemptions, occupancy rates and types of hotels do matter.

A study by World Tourism Organisation (1988) indicated that it was common in ìtourist countriesî to get between 10-25 percent of their fiscal revenues from tourism.[6] The proportion may go up to 50 percent for smaller and specialised tourist countries such as Bahamas. On average, 10 percent of gross tourism receipts go to government revenues in the Caribbean countries (Bryden 1973) compared to 20 percent reported in Tunisia and Kenya. The figures may however, be much less and sometimes negative after taking into account expenditures necessary to support the tourist sector, including import leakages (although these may lead to extra government revenue) and public investment (infrastructure).

Obviously the fiscal impact of tourism may differ from country to country, depending on national policies but also on the linkages with the rest of the economy and the degree of maturity of the tourism sector. Enclave type of tourist centres where most supplies come from abroad and with mostly foreign employees, are expected to have minimal impact on host country economies and fiscal revenues. Also early periods of tourism development are expected to have high leakages and therefore minimal revenues. On average, it is estimated that about 55 percent of tourism expenditures remains outside the destination country, rising to 75 percent in specific cases such as the Gambia and Commonwealth Caribbean, but as little as 25 percent for large economies such as India (Ashley, et al 2000).

---

[6] According to Bryden (1973), a ìtourist countryî is one in which tourism accounts for more than 10 percent of foreign exchange earnings or over 5 percent of GDP.

There are also indirect incomes and employment generated from tourist purchases outside the hotel business, which sometimes may be more important than the direct effects, but once again are hard(er) to estimate. de Kadt (1979) indicates that tourists usually spend less than two-thirds of their expenditures on typical tourist hotels/restaurants. Therefore, the rest is spent elsewhere, on souvenirs and transport services, and on indirect services provided to tourists, such as food and other items supplied to hotels and restaurants, construction facilities, capital goods and the tax collected on this expenditure.

The distributional consequences of tourism are also important. One can ask, for instance, who are the major beneficiaries, national and foreign, and which groups within nations, maybe losers in the process of economic change? A comparison of what tourists spend at home, before departure (on travel and hotel bookings), and what they spend abroad, in host countries, is also revealing. Maina-wa- Kinyatti (1980) argued that while tourism does bring in foreign exchange, much of the profit is returned to the foreign investors who own most tourist facilities; further, it may shift development away from industries that might permit increased self-reliance. But even if foreigners benefit most from international tourism, the benefits for poor countries may still be sizeable especially where local communities have access to markets for commodities purchased by tourists such as handicraft, tour operation and souvenirs.

Tourism will contribute to poverty reduction if it creates new jobs and provides incomes. From the literature it is clear that it does so, and that often particular groups (youth, women) do benefit. One would like to know more, in this respect, about the types of jobs that are created, the levels of skills required, recruitment policies, involvement of locals, training facilities, etc. Job creation will have to be compared with the number of losers as a result of tourism expansion, and the extent to which losers are able to grasp new income opportunities.

3.0 TOURISM IN TANZANIA

3.1 POLICY FRAMEWORK

Until 1991, Tanzania did not have a definite tourism policy. Tourism in Tanzania (Mainland) evolved through various stages and periods. During the first decade of independence, tourism was not viewed as a priority sector for development. The focus of the government was only on wildlife conservation, putting little emphasis on actual utilisation and promotion.

14

In 1971, the Tanzania Tourist Corporation (TTC) was established to promote and market tourism within and outside the country. This paid off as more tourists visited Tanzania in 1972 (199,200 tourists) compared to 1971 (68,400 tourists). However, with the after effects of the drought of 1974, the Uganda War of 1979 and the economic crisis that emerged from the late 1970s to the mid 1980s, tourism industry did not perform impressively.

The tourism policy of 1991 (revised in 1999), places emphasis on the promotion of private sector investment, environmental conservation and consumer protection. The main objectives of the sector are outlined as:

(i)   to maximise tourism's contribution to the country's development through increased foreign exchange earnings, employment creation, human resource development and rural development; and

(ii)   to ensure the conservation of tourism attractions, preservation of the environment and the sustainable development of the tourism industry.

In Zanzibar, tourism has been encouraged as a main source of foreign exchange and therefore economic growth. Both local and foreign private companies and individuals are encouraged to invest in the sector. Unfortunately, there is no policy in place. The government has attracted expanding tourist entrepreneurs and tourists. However, confronted with mass tourism, Zanzibaris experience limited access to and control over their coastal zones, partly due to lack of institutional framework for the sector.

3.2 TOURISM TRENDS IN TANZANIA

The reforms that started in 1986 in Tanzania Mainland, and particularly the increased private sector participation, had positive impact on the tourism industry. Apart from the Tourism Policy of 1991 (revised in 1999), the strengthening of investment incentives under the Tanzania Investment Act of 1997 acted in a positive way in attracting investors into the sector. The number of projects approved by the Tanzania Investment Centre (TIC) kept on growing from 31 projects in 1997 to 229 projects in 2000. However, as not all approved projects do materialise and therefore not all employment opportunities are generated, the actual employment created cannot be ascertained.

Tourism became the fastest growing industry in Tanzania in the 1990s, after decades of stagnation. It is a sign of Tanzania joining the world, where tourism is one of the largest industries (second after oil). Tourist arrivals, for example, increased from 103,000 in 1986 to 153,000 in 1990 and reached 627,000 tourists in 1999. Tourist earnings also increased from US$ 20 million to US$ 65 million and US$ 733 million during the same periods. The earnings increased from $10 to 20 million, annually, in the 1970s and the early 1980s, to $60 million in 1989. There was also a more than ten-fold increase in ten years time from 1989 to 1999, and even a doubling in the last four years. The annual growth rate of tourism since 1985 has been over 30 percent[7], showing how tourism is positively responding to the reforms. Problems in Kenya, negatively affecting the flow of tourists, also played a role in increasing the flow of tourists to Tanzania.

Unfortunately, tourism did not perform well during year 2000 and 2001. Inflows of tourists declined in year 2000 with marginal increase in year 2001. However, tourist earnings improved marginally in year 2000 but declined in year 2001 (Table 1 and Figure 2).

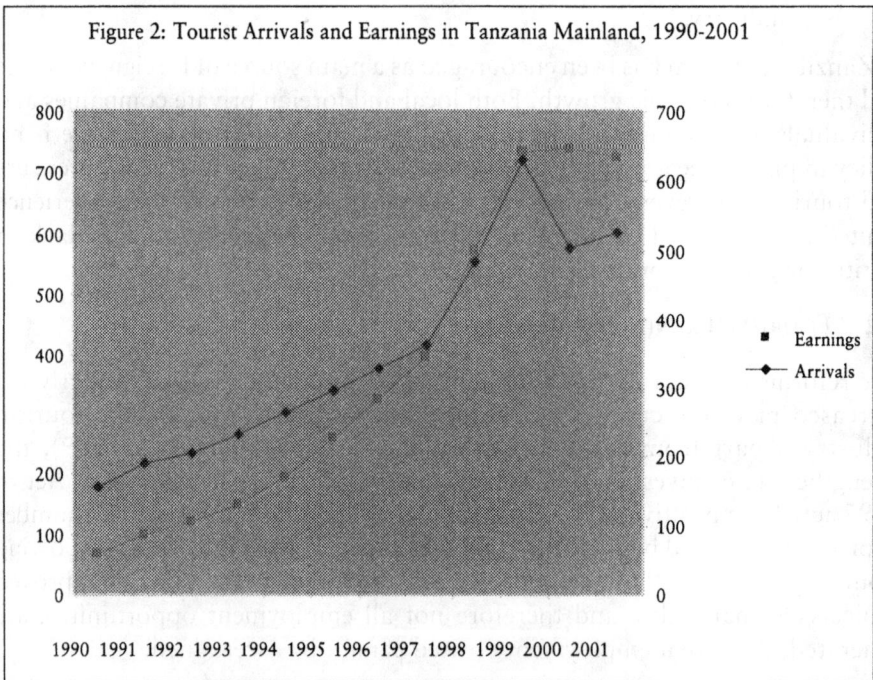

Figure 2: Tourist Arrivals and Earnings in Tanzania Mainland, 1990-2001

Source: Data from Economic Survey, 2002.

7 See Ndulu et al (1998).

Table 1: Tourists, Hotels, Earnings and Employment in Tanzania, 1990-2001

Description	1990	1991	1992	1993	1994	1995	1996	1997	1998	1999	2000	2001
Tourists Arrivals (000)	153	187	202	230	262	295	326	360	482	627	502	525
Tourists in Hotels (000)		172	188	216	239	268	296	345	457	565	480	501
Number of Hotels		205	207	198	208	210	212	213	215	321	326	329
Total bed-nights (000)	1223	1031	1126	1320	1455	1663	1866	2243	2944	3381	3837	5549
Average number of bed-nights per visit (days)		7.0	7.0	7.1	7.1	7.2	7.3	7.5	7.6	7.7		
Average hotel occupancy rate/year		56	56	56	56	57	56	56	60	64	54	59
Average daily expenditure per tourist (US$)		72	85	90	103	122	135	145	156	152	184	173
Average Earnings per tourist (US$)		507	595	638	734	879	988	1090	1182	1169	1473	1169
Total Earnings (US$ Mln)		95	120	147	192	259	322	392	570	733	739	725
Employees in Tourist Sector (000)	65	45	50	66	86	96	100	110	132	148	156	157

Source: The Economic Survey (various), Presidentís Office; Planning and Privatisation.

17

Average earnings per tourist in Tanzania are also high, increasing from an average of US$ 500 in the early 1990s to over US$ 1000 towards the end of the decade. This compares favourably with the average for Africa that is between US$ 300 and US$ 400 (WTO various).

Tourism accounted for about 60 percent of all exports of goods and services in 1999 compared to only 12 percent in 1990, more than all traditional exports together (the six crops include coffee, tea, cotton, tobacco, cashew nuts and sisal), and ten to twenty four times more than (official) exports of minerals and of manufactured goods (each). Earnings from tourism contributed 9 percent to the national GDP in 1999, compared with only 1.5 percent in 1990 and around 0.3 percent in the early 1980s. And although tourism increases imports, its revenues alone now finance more than 40 percent of all imports.[8] The over 600,000 arrivals for 1999 (Figure 2) also mean a twelve-fold increase compared to the 50,000 annual visitors in the early 1980s.[9]

Generally, Tanzania is rapidly catching up with leading African tourist destinations, taking a sixth position (in earnings) in 1997 after South Africa, Morocco, Tunisia, Mauritius and Kenya, but number eight in arrivals, after Zimbabwe and Botswana.[10] While Kenya still had 951,000 visitors in 1998 and Tanzania only half of that (482,000 visitors), its earnings ($570 million) surpassed those of Kenya ($358 million) for the first time in that year. Some other African countries have managed to attract many tourists and increased substantially their earnings from tourism. South Africa for instance, earns over $ 2 billion from tourism, with over 5 million arrivals per year. Tanzania, too with her great tourist potentials could increase substantially its earnings from tourism.

Zanzibar also has witnessed a growing tourist sector. Doubling its tourist arrivals since 1990 from 42,000 to 86,000 tourists in 1997. International visitation increased at an average annual rate of 16 percent during the first ten years since the start of the economic reforms of 1987. The economic reforms had envisaged tourism as one of the major areas for future economic growth and employment creation. Annual shifts in visitation have ranged from a 60 percent rise in 1988 soon after liberalisation, to the only decline in 1994 (of 40 percent), most likely a result of political conflicts in neighbouring countries and publicity

---

[8] See Luvanga and Bol (1999).
[9] See URT (2000).
[10] See Luvanga and Bol (1999).

18

about Ebola virus. In general, prospects look good as Africa is attracting more tourists every year, also relatively compared to other destinations (e.g. Asia).

From 1995 up to 2000 tourist arrivals in Zanzibar increased significantly from 56,415 tourists to 97,165 tourists. Most impressive growth was registered between 1999 and 2000 when tourist arrivals recorded an 11.8 percent growth in inflows. Specifically, the rapid jump in the number of tourist arrivals from the year 1997 was largely a result of the open door policy. Foreign earnings also increased (Figure 3). The monthly room occupancy rates ranged between 20 percent and 48 percent during 1999 and 2000. Tourism is estimated to contribute at least US$ 5 million annually in direct spending and hotel levy brings in a monthly average of US$ 11,000 on the Island (Zanzibar Tourism Draft Policy, 1998). This gives an indication that Zanzibarís diversified product mix has been gaining widespread demand in the global world market.

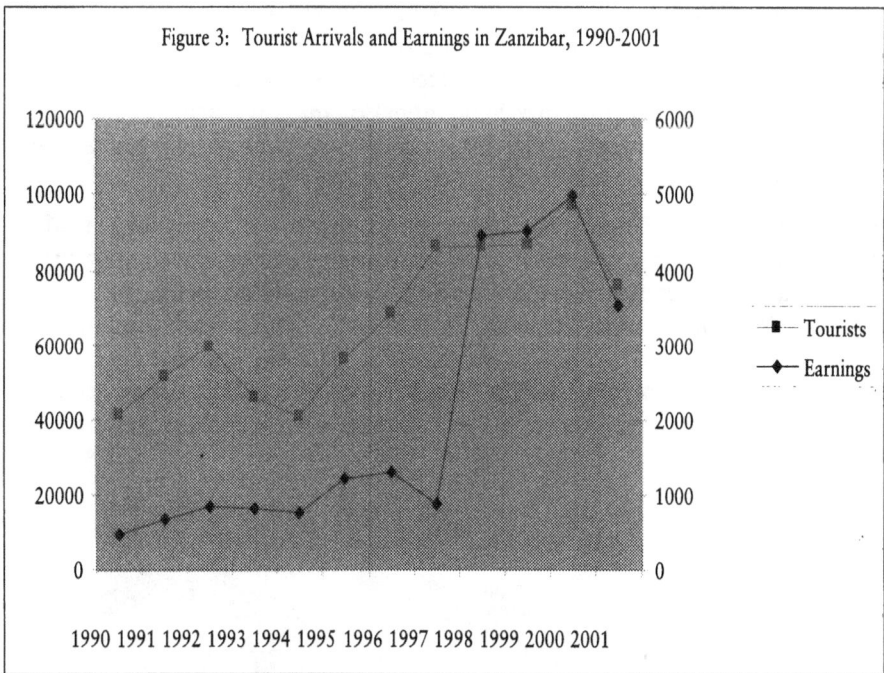

Figure 3: Tourist Arrivals and Earnings in Zanzibar, 1990-2001

Source: Data from Zanzibar Statistical Database

The attraction of Stone Town as one of the World Heritage sites anchors Zanzibarís image and promotions. Historic sites such as Beit El Ajaab (House

19

of Wonders), Old Fort, Livingstone House, newly restored Old Dispensary, Anglican Cathedral on the site of the former slave market, Tippu Tip House, Maruhubi Palace and other ruins of the former sultans, are important attractions to tourists. Additionally, Zanzibarís tranquil, palm ñ fringed beaches are well-known, but the menu of marine recreation activities has also expanded to include scuba diving, snorkelling, deep-sea fishing, sailboat charters, dolphin watching and visits to the offshore islets and coral reefs.

Unfortunately, both Tanzania Mainland and Zanzibar did not perform well during year 2001. In Tanzania Mainland there was a modest increase in tourist inflows from 501,669 in 2000 to 525,122 in 2001, an increase of 5 percent. In spite of the increase in number of tourists, revenue collection from tourism decreased from US$739 million in 2000 to US$ 725 million in 2001. In Zanzibar, both tourist inflows and revenue collection from tourism sector decreased. The poor performance of tourism sector in 2001 is attributed to the effect of September 11, 2001 terrorist attacks in the USA which disrupted tourism activities in the country (and other parts of the World). In the case of Tanzania, the tourism business was affected because the attack happened at the end of the second season (July-September) of mass tourism, where a big number of organised tourists visit the country especially the high spending tourists from the USA.

However, important indicators of the size and direction of demand for tourist services are the number of tourists coming to the country as well as the gross foreign exchange earnings realized. Generally, tourism performance in Tanzania during the 1990s has been impressive (Table 2)[11]. The growth rates in both arrivals and earnings for 1990-2000 were high, with earnings taking an upper hand. In Mainland Tanzania, growth rates for arrivals and earnings were 13.2 percent and 25.0 respectively, while for Zanzibar were 8.3 percent and 22.6 percent respectively.

---

[11] The break in year 2000 is intended to reflect the effects of the September 11, 2001 on Tourism sector.

Table 2: Tourist Arrivals and Earnings Growth Rates in Tanzania, 1990-2001 (percent)

Period	Tanzania Mainland		Zanzibar	
	Arrivals	Earnings	Arrivals	Earnings
1990-1995	12.7	26.3	1.5	13.5
1996-2000	14.2	22.9	0.8	43.0
1996-2001	10.4	17.7	2.4	29.0
1990-2000	13.2	25.0	8.3	22.6
1990-2001	12.3	23.4	7.1	21.1

Source: Economic Survey and Zanzibar Statistical Database

4.0 ANALYSIS OF RESULTS

4.1 INTRODUCTION

Both positive and negative impacts of tourism on poverty alleviation are analysed in this section using data and information gathered from the survey. Such analysis is deemed important because it is now generally recognised that as tourism expands and bring wider economic benefits (including generation of income, employment, revenue and foreign exchange), it also potentially, results into a disturbing array of social environmental impacts. Understanding these issues is crucial for proper planning and managing of sustainable tourism development, which in turn requires that the social and environmental implications of tourism development must be integrated into development policy.

4.2 COVERAGE

The results presented, are based on survey data collected from two regions of Mainland Tanzania (Arusha and Coast) and one region of Zanzibar Island (North Unguja). The number, proportion and structure of the surveyed households is shown in Table 3.

Table 3: Households Coverage for the Study Areas

Region	District	Village/Ward	Total H/Hs	Surveyed H/Hs	% of H/Hs Surveyed	% of H/Hs in Total Surveyed	Sex of Head of Household M	Sex of Head of Household F
Arusha	Monduli	Mto wa Mbu Barabarani*	700	65	9.3	23.1	53	12
	Karatu	Kilima moja*	590	25	4.2	8.9	23	2
Sub-Total			1290	90	7.0	32.0	76	14
Coast	Bagamoyo	Dunda**	2726	74	2.7	26.3	70	4
		Magomeni**	2559	22	0.9	7.8	17	5
Sub-Total			5285	96	1.8	34.1	87	9
North Unguja	North B	Kiwengwa-Cairo*	71	28	39.4	10.0	26	2
		Kiwengwa-Gulioni*	51	20	39.2	7.1	19	1
		Kiwengwa-Kumbaurembo*	119	47	39.5	16.8	40	7
Sub-Total			241	95	39.4	33.9	85	10
Grand-Total			6816	281	4.1	100.0	248	33

Note: * = village
      ** = ward

Source: Survey Data, 2001/2002.

According to Table 3, in the two villages of Arusha 90 (7.0 percent) out of the total 1,290 households were surveyed while in the two wards of Coast Region (Bagamoyo) 96 (1.6 percent) of the total 5,285 households were surveyed. In North Unguja, 95 (39.4 percent) of the total 241 households were surveyed. The percentage for the surveyed households out of the total households in the area of study in Bagamoyo is relatively lower compared to that of Arusha and Zanzibar. This is partly attributed to the fact that in Arusha and Zanzibar the reference is with respect to ì villageî while in Bagamoyo it is ì wardî. Nevertheless, the coverage of the three areas was more or less equal with each area contributing around one third of the surveyed households. Further analysis of the data reveals that most of the total surveyed households, 248 or 88 percent (out of 281) were male headed.

4.3 ECONOMIC ACTIVITIES OF SURVEYED HOUSEHOLDS

The surveyed areas are basically rural areas and hence in addition to tourist related socio-economic activities there are several agricultural related economic activities. Few members of the surveyed households were also undertaking other non-farm activities. The various economic activities undertaken in the areas of study are shown in Table 4.

Table 4: Major Economic Activities in Study Areas

S/N	Economic Activity	Mto wa Mbu		Bagamoyo		North Unguja		Total	
		No.	Percent	No.	Percent	No.	Percent	No.	Percent
1.	Farming/Livestock	67	25.9	12	6.5	58	28.3	137	21.1
2.	Business (incl. Crop & cloth selling	24	9.3	9	4.8	20	9.8	53	8.1
3.	Curio and other shop	55	21.2	18	9.7	20	9.8	93	14.3
4.	Handcraft	15	5.8	47	25.3	13	6.3	75	11.5
5.	Fishing	0	0.0	6	3.2	28	13.6	34	5.2
6.	Tour operator, Guide, Taxi	25	9.7	42	22.6	34	16.6	101	15.5
8.	Fruit selling	19	7.3	7	3.8	0	0.0	26	4.0
9.	Government employees	6	2.3	3	1.6	7	3.4	16	2.5
10.	Hotel employees	7	2.7	14	7.5	21	10.2	42	6.5
11.	Private sector employees	11	4.2	14	7.5	2	1.0	27	4.2
12.	Food vendor	3	1.1	0	0.0	0	0.0	3	0.5
13.	Entertainment (culture, music)	25	9.7	10	5.4	0	0.0	35	5.4
14.	Small business e.g. Shoe shine	2	0.8	4	2.1	2	1.0	8	1.2
	Total	259	100.0	186	100.0	205	100.0	650	100.0

Overall, out of the eleven economic activities identified in the areas of study, agriculture (farming and livestock) is the most practiced by residents. This is not surprising given that the areas of study have a rural setting. But if all tourist related activities are grouped together, then they dominate in the surveyed areas. Tourist related activities such as tour operation, curio shops and handcraft are important. However, there are differences in participation rates in these activities among the different areas of study. Participation rates for tour operation are 9.7 percent in Mto wa Mbu, 22.6 percent in Bagamoyo and 16.6 percent in North Unguja. Those for curio shops are 21.2 percent, 9.7 percent and 9.8 percent respectively while those for handcraft are 5.8 percent, 25.3 percent and 6.3 percent respectively.

Further desegregation indicates the type of specific tourist related activities in each location. In Mto wa mbu and Kilimamoja villages in Arusha the tourist related activities that appear to be attracting more people include fruit selling, curio shops and tour operating. Cultural tourism was also observed to be important in Mto wa Mbu. As the incomes from this type of tourism goes direct to the performer (individual), it should be of significance towards poverty alleviation. Magomeni and Dunda villages in Bagamoyo, key tourist related activities include handcraft, tour operating and tour guide and paid employment in hotels. Cultural tourism is also gaining importance in these areas. In Kiwengwa area in Zanzibar the leading tourism related activities are mainly tour guide, carving, curio shop and sea sport/beach. Participating in these activities forms the basis through which the locals can benefit from tourism.

Participation in different activities was also analysed according to age and gender for all residents of the surveyed households. Patterns of participation in those activities by age and gender are shown in Table 5.

Table 5: Participation in Different Activities in Surveyed Areas by Age & Gender

| | AGE CATEGORIES | | | | | | | | | | Total | |
| | <15 | | 15 ñ 21 | | 22 ñ 30 | | 31 ñ 50 | | Above 50 | | | |
	M	F	M	F	M	F	M	F	M	F	M	F
Too young/child	53	50	-	-	-	-	-	-	-	-	53	50
Student	91	88	31	37	2	0	0	0	0	0	124	125
Tourist related	1	2	39	6	125	29	103	30	9	2	277	69
Farming/livestock	1	1	4	13	9	37	14	35	13	10	41	96
Fishing	0	1	2	1	7	3	15	0	5	0	29	5
Paid employee ñ Govt	0	0	0	0	2	2	8	3	0	1	10	6
Paid employee ñPrivate	2	1	4	2	8	5	3	2	0	0	17	10
Self employment	4	2	5	1	3	4	7	5	1	0	20	12
Unpaid family helper	5	1	5	7	6	4	3	3	0	0	19	15
Household worker	0	0	0	5	0	23	0	8	0	2	0	38
Unemployed	0	0	6	5	5	2	0	1	0	0	11	8
Not active	0	0	0	0	0	0	1	1	4	9	5	10
Total	157	146	93	77	167	109	154	88	32	24	606	444

Source: Survey Data, 2001/2002.

Participation in different activities by age and gender also reveal that most of the residents in the surveyed areas are in tourist related activities, and farming/livestock. Students also constitute a significant proportion. However, with regard to adults, age brackets 22-30 and 31-50 years are mostly involved in tourist related activities and farming for both males and females. Overall, 346 or 50.6 percent of the economically active residents participated in tourist related activities with gender division of 80 percent for males and 20 percent for females. However, males dominate in tourism related activities whereas females dominate in agriculture. Household work is observed to be exclusively for women. Both males and females are more or less equally represented in their capacities as being too young/child, student and paid employees.

As already pointed earlier, age brackets of 22-30 and 31-50 years dominated with participation rates of 44.5 percent and 38.4 percent respectively. A summary of participation in tourism related activities is presented in Figure 4.

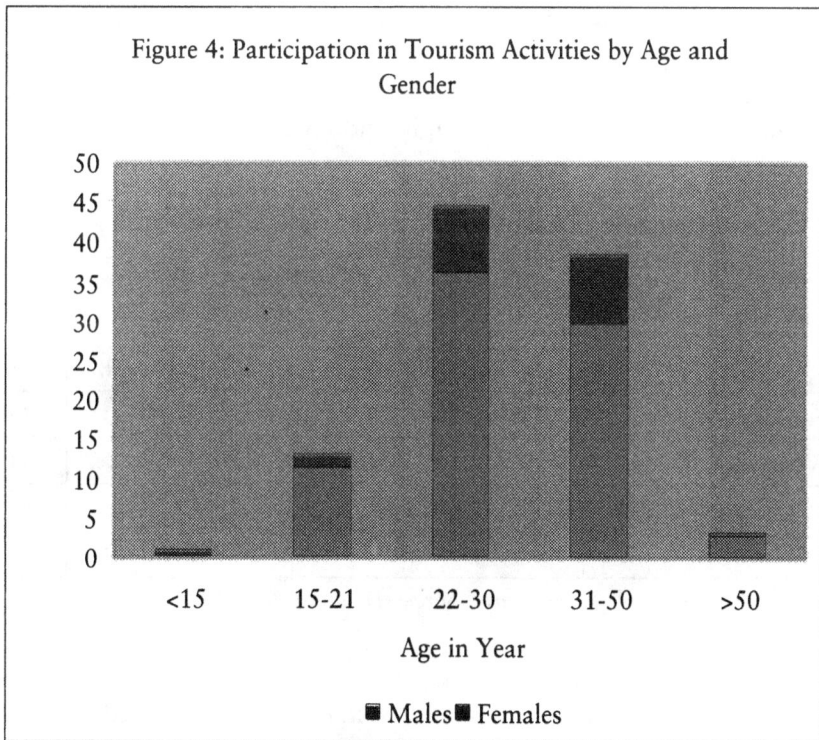

Figure 4: Participation in Tourism Activities by Age and Gender

Source: Survey Data, 2001/2002.

27

4.4 IMPACT OF TOURISM ON POVERTY ALLEVIATION

Tourism activities can affect poverty alleviation positively or negatively. Positive contributions may be registered through employment creation, income generation, increased asset ownership, contribution to basic needs and contributions to community benefits. However, together with benefits, linkages and multipliers, tourism effects may result in some costs or negative impacts. These may be seen through environmental problems, cultural pollution, immoral behaviour and conflicts with other socio economic activities.

4.4.1 *Positive Impacts*

4.4.1.1 On Employment Levels

A number of employment generation activities have shown an increasing trend in all three areas of study. It was observed that a significant number of people in the surveyed households are employed in campsites, guesthouses and tourist hotels and restaurants. This is an indication that tourism activities are important for the livelihood of the members of these households. Table 6 presents the structure of employment in the surveyed hotels, restaurants, and guesthouses and campsites by position and origin and Figure 5 by origin.

Table 6: Structure of Employment in Operating Hotels in Areas of Study

Origin of Employee	Position of Employee									
	Managers		Heads of Dept		Supervisors		Service Staff		Total	
	No.	%	No.	%	No.	%	No.	%	No.	%
Foreigners	22	34.4	20	30.3	16	16.5	0	0.0	58	5.2
Within the Village	9	14.1	5	7.6	5	5.2	272	30.7	291	26.1
Other regions	33	51.5	41	62.1	76	78.3	615	69.3	765	68.7
Total	64	100.0	66	100.0	97	100.0	887	100.0	1114	100.0

Source: Survey Data, 2001/2002.

According to Table 6 employment generation in hotels for locals is in the lower cadres. For example, the hotels covered in this study employed a total of 1,114 employees. However, the majority of the employees from within the villages were concentrated on the service staff cadre, involving 272 employees (30.7

percent) of all employees in the cadre. This is the highest concentration for employees from within the villages and is among the lowest cadres in the employment structure. In the higher cadres they were marginally represented. For example, in the managerial cadre, there were only 9 (14.1 percent) out of 64 managers. On the other hand, foreigners occupied higher cadres of employment, such as managers (34.4percent), heads of departments (30.3percent) and supervisors (16.5percent). Even where Tanzanians were employed in the higher cadres, the preference seems to have been from outside the location of the hotel (other parts of Tanzania). None of the foreigners were employed as service staff.

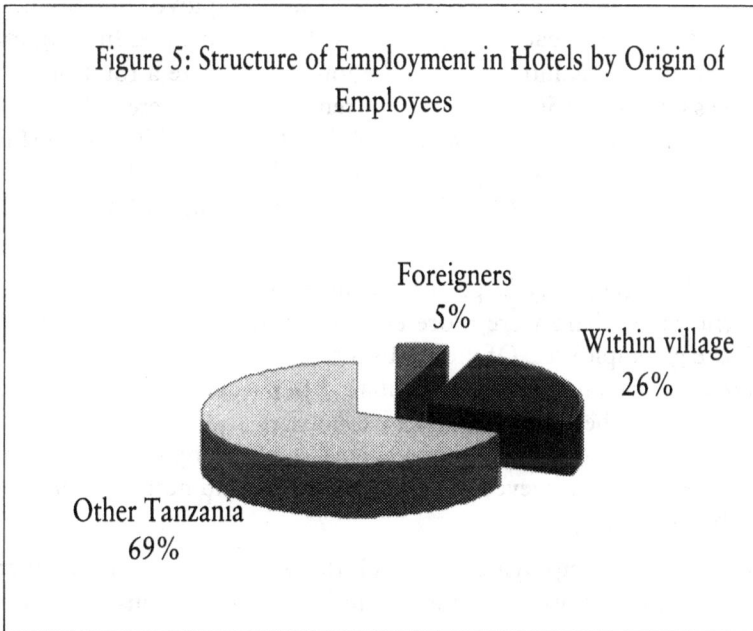

Figure 5: Structure of Employment in Hotels by Origin of Employees

Foreigners 5%

Within village 26%

Other Tanzania 69%

Source: Table 6

The concentration of Tanzanians on low levels of employment and foreigners on higher levels appear to be a common phenomenon in the Tanzanian tourist industry. Apparently, this may partly be a reflection of the skilled and unskilled nature of hotel jobs. As most Tanzanians lack the prerequisite skills/training, they tend to be employed in menial, unskilled positions such as waiters, room cleaners and kitchen keepers. Concentration in low employment opportunities is generally correlated to low pay.

Although most of the Tanzanian employees are on the lower cadres, generally the hotels offer significant employment opportunities to locals (both men and women). Out of the total of 1,114 employees in hotels, 1,056 (94.8 percent) were Tanzanians. In terms of gender, male employees were 672 (63.6 percent) while females were 384 (36.4 percent).

Employment levels at each location of the study revealed that in Mto wa Mbu Barabarani and Kilimamoja villages (Arusha Region), there is no foreign employee. However, there was significant local participation of both males and females. The majority of these employees in the two villages were employed by Lake Manyara Hotel, a major tourist hotel in the area. Lake Manyara Hotel alone employs 80 males and 31 females. The rest were employed in small hotels, restaurants and campsites each employing less than 10 people. In Magomeni and Dunda wards of Bagamoyo (Coast Region), there were a total of 285 of such employees involving 150 males and 135 females. There were only 4 foreign employees. Two tourist hotels of Paradise Holiday Resort and Livingstone Hotel dominated with a total of 140 employees. Each of the hotels had 70 employees with a gender distribution of 40 males and 30 females; and 37 males and 33 females respectively.

In Zanzibar, where relatively large foreign investments in hotels have taken place in recent years, there were more employees in terms of total numbers, female and foreign employees. Of the 1,114 total employees, 644 (57.8 percent) of them were employed in hotels in Zanzibar. In terms of gender, 68.5 percent and 31.5 percent) of the 644 employees were males and females respectively. 54 employees (8.3 percent) were foreign employees compared to only four foreign employees in the surveyed areas of Bagamoyo and none in Arusha (See Table 7 on the next page).

An interesting aspect of employment in hotels (for Zanzibar)[12], is the distinction of employees between those in operation and those under construction. The hotel owners were asked how many of the employees were from the local village(s) and how many were from outside the immediate area. The results revealed that although in absolute terms hotels under construction and operation recruited more employees from outside the immediate area, relatively, hotels under construction recruited more employees from outside the village than operating hotels did. These results corroborate those of Sulaiman (1996) (See

---

[12] Only in Kiwengwa (Zanzibar), where some good data on hotels under construction was obtained.

Table 8). Arguably, these employees are unskilled labour. As most of the people of Zanzibar are fishermen, they appear to be unwilling to accept construction work for wages that people from agricultural areas inland, or the unemployed from Zanzibar Town, will work for. Fishing, although not without its problems, still provides a relatively good income by the standards of rural Zanzibar (Sulaiman, 1996). However, lack of the required skills in the construction industry also played its part. Most of the people from within the area had no skills and experience with the construction industry.

Table 7: Employment Levels in Hotels by Area of Study, Citizenship and Gender (Number of employees)

S/n	Area of Study	Employment					
		Tanzanians		Foreigners		Total	
		M	F	M	F	M	F
	Arusha Region						
1.	Mto wa Mbu Barabarani:	28	23	0	0	28	23
2.	Kalimamoja:	90	44	0	0	90	44
	Sub-Total (1. +2.)	118	67	0	0	118	67
	Coast Region						
3.	Magomeni:	92	80	4	0	96	80
4.	Dunda	54	55	0	0	54	55
	Sub-Total (3. +4.)	146	135	4	0	150	135
	North Unguja						
5.	Kiwengwa-Cairo	6	2	0	0	6	0
6.	Gulioni	395	174	33	21	428	195
7.	Kumba Urembo	7	6	-	-	7	6
	Sub-Total (5+6+7)	408	182	33	21	441	203
	Grand Total	672	384	37	21	709	405

Source: Survey Data, 2001/2002.

Table 8: Origin of Employees Involved in Operation and Construction of Hotels in Zanzibar, 1996 and 2002

Condition of Hotels	Employees from					
	Village	Other Unguja	Other Tanzania	Village (Kiwengwa)	Other Unguja	Other Tanzania
	1996			2002		
Operating	145	198	-	93	132	365
Construction	132	372	57	69	153	44

Source: Sulaiman (1996) for 1996; and Survey Data, 2001/2002 for 2002.

4.4.1.2 On Income Levels

Getting accurate income levels of interviewees is usually not easy as has been the case for this study. It was not easy for instance, to get accurate data on salaries for employees of tourist hotels, restaurants, guesthouses and campsites. The study, therefore, reports in this section only the number of people, by income groups who received incomes from various tourism related activities. This reflects how impacts of tourism is being felt in the areas of the study through backward and forward linkages between tourism and other sectors of the economy such as agriculture, transport and other services.

Table 9: Number of People Receiving Incomes From Tourism Related Activities by Income Group, (1999 and 2001)

	Income Range						
	1-100,000	100,001-500,000	500,001-1,000,000	1,000,001-5,000,000	5,000,001-10,000,000	Above 10,000,000	Total
1999							
Tour Operating	2	18	9	7	0	1	37
Handcraft	3	10	15	3	0	0	31
Hotel Business	0	5	3	0	0	0	8
Supplying Commodities	6	10	5	1	0	0	22
Taxi Business	0	0	4	3	0	0	7
Curio Shops	5	12	13	10	0	0	40
Other Tourism Related	8	20	14	15	0	1	58
Total	24	75	63	39	0	2	203
2001							
Tour Operating	5	14	7	7	1	1	35
Handcraft	2	14	13	3	0	0	32
Hotel Business	0	5	6	1	0	0	12
Supplying Commodities	7	12	3	0	1	0	23
Taxi Business	0	1	4	3	1	0	9
Curio Shops	10	18	9	11	1	0	49
Other Tourism Related	9	27	22	16	0	1	75
Total	33	91	64	41	4	2	235

Source: Survey Data, 2001/2002.

According to Table 9, tourism related activities are important sources of income especially for people within the income group ranging from Tshs 100,001 to 5,000,000. There are also a substantial number of small income earners (between Tshs 1 to 100,000) who rely on tourism related activities. Within two years the number of people who receive income from tourism related activities increased by about 16 percent, from 203(in 1999) to 235 (in 2001). However, the general pattern of contribution of incomes from tourism to households did not reflect an (upward trend) increase. But the rather rapid growth in the number of those receiving incomes from tourism related activities is an indication of the growing importance of tourism in the areas of the study.

Further analysis of incomes from tourism related activities indicate that some activities provide high levels of incomes to operators. The range in the different activities for the maximum is from Tshs 1,200,000 to Tshs 12,000,000 per annum, whereas that for the minimum is from Tshs 20,000 to Tshs 1,800,000.

4.4.1.3 Tourism Employment and Income Multipliers[13]

The positive impacts of tourism can also be measured through employment and income multipliers. Tourism employment multipliers summarize either the direct, indirect and induced employment generated by an additional sum of tourism expenditure in the destination economy, or the ratio of the increase in direct employment to the increase in overall employment. In either case, however, the higher the multiplier coefficient, the greater the amount of additional employment that will be created by a given increase in tourism expenditure. Apart from the direct employment created by tourism related hotels, restaurants, guest houses and campsites in the surveyed areas, there are also indirect employment opportunities created mainly by the linkages of tourism to other sectors. There are for example, several people who are engaged in various tourist related activities such as tour guide, tour operating, curio shops operation, fruit selling to tourists, agricultural crop/fruit and vegetable supplies to tourists hotels, food vending, hand craft and cultural/music entertainment. All these are important sources of employment.

On the other hand, the conceptual basis of the tourism income multipliers is the assumption that a direct injection of cash into a destination economy, for example, through spending by tourists, will result in increased incomes for the suppliers of tourism services (direct incomes). A proportion of the additional

---

[13] Due to poor quality of data, figures for the relevant multipliers are not reported.

incomes will be saved while the remainder will be either spent on replenishing stocks or redistributed to tourism employees in the form of wages (indirect incomes). Also, a proportion of these indirect incomes will in turn be saved or spent on consumer goods and services, thereby generating induced incomes in the economy. Of course, at each stage of expenditure it is assumed that a proportion of expenditure is on imports, resulting in a leakage of expenditure from the local economy.

4.4.1.4 Increased Asset Ownership

Increased ownership of assets is an important reflection of how the poor are raising their abilities to get out of poverty. Interviewees were asked to provide information on how tourism affected their assets/resources that are important for poverty alleviation. Assets/Resources that were considered are Physical Assets, Human Resources, Natural Resources and Social Capital. The results indicate that tourism had significant positive impact on physical and human resources assets. In these two types of assets the responses show that positive impacts of tourism outweigh negative impacts by far. The most important specific impacts identified include the acquisition of cash, capital, consumer durables, equity investment, training, employment opportunities and good use and management of resources.

On the other hand, both the positive and negative impacts of tourism are significant and more or less balanced with regard to natural resources and social capital. Whereas, there are positive impacts there are also significant negative impacts. These (marginally also mentioned under physical and human resources) include high competition in the use of resources (assets), loss of access to resources, exhaustion of resources, conflicts with investors and distortion of traditional culture (See figure 6 and 7).

Figure 6: Impact of Tourism on People's Assets/Resources by Type of Asset

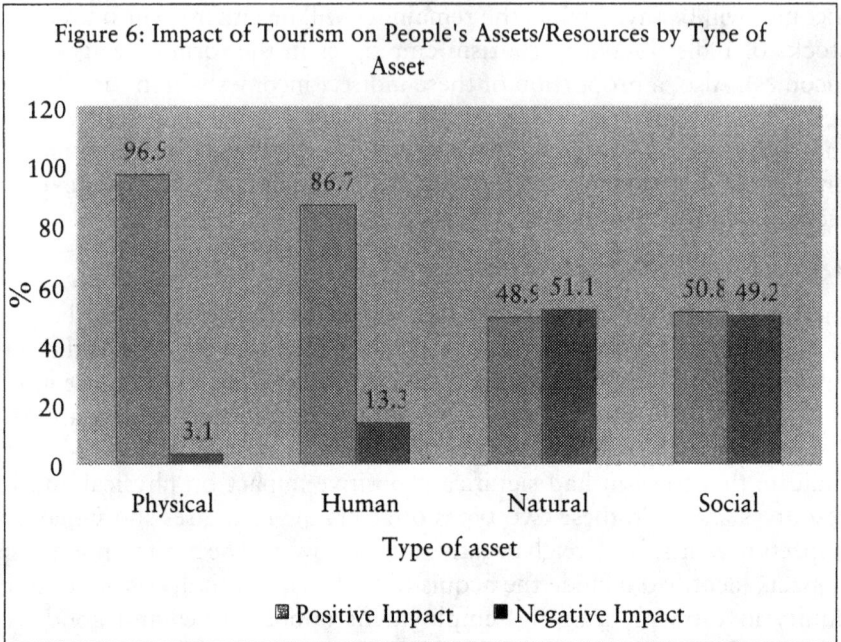

Source: Survey Data, 2001/2002

Figure 7: Overall Impact of Tourism on People's Assets/Resources

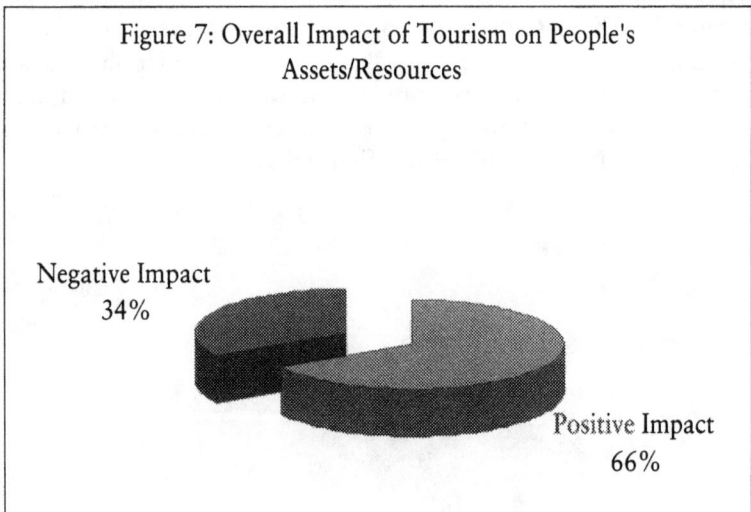

Source: Survey Data, 2001/2002

4.4.1.5   Contribution of Tourism Activities to Basic Needs

Interviewees were asked to provide information on the contribution of the various economic activities to their basic needs. The basic needs were grouped into immediate needs (food, water and energy) and indirect needs/assets (cash, goods for barter exchange, reserves, inputs to production and social capital). Table 10 presents a summary of the information provided in this regard.

Table 10:   Contribution of Tourism to Basic Needs in the Surveyed Areas (Number of Reporting households)

Basic Needs	Arusha			Bagamoyo			North B		
	*	**	***	*	**	***	*	**	***
Immediate needs									
Food	10	7	1	21	29	5	2	20	13
Water, Energy	2	0	0	23	6	4	25	4	3
Indirect Needs/Assets									
Cash	12	29	31	26	20	18	20	28	19
Goods for barter exchange	1	0	0	0	1	0	0	0	0
Reserves & Investment	10	9	2	4	1	1	8	5	2
Inputs to production	24	8	3	12	9	1	7	4	1
Cultural and Intangible Assets	9	1	0	1	0	0	0	0	0
Social capital community organization	3	4	0	2	1	1	1	1	1

Note: * indicates a minor or indirect contribution

   ** Indicates moderate contribution

   *** Indicates that tourism makes a major contribution to a need.

Source: Survey Data, 2001/2002.

According to Table 10 above tourism has been contributing to the accessibility of various basic needs. In all areas of study earnings from participation in tourist related activities have been helping the locals to buy food, to boost their cash incomes, to maintain some savings, to make investments and to purchase inputs required in production in several economic activities. This linkage forms the basis for further analysis on the role which tourism can play in poverty alleviation in the areas of our study.

4.4.1.6 Community Benefits

Some of the community benefits in tourist localities have been the improvement in infrastructure and social services. Although there were complaints from tour operators of bad roads in Mto wa Mbu (Arusha) and Kiwengwa (North Zanzibar), some improvements were observed to have taken place. Indeed, even at community level, residents in those areas reported that with tourism development, roads were now being frequently repaired/rehabilitated than they previously used to be. Further, construction of the road from Dar es Salaam to Bagamoyo to a tarmac level is almost complete. Apart from improving accessibility to tourist attractions, when completed this road will also benefit the residents of Bagamoyo and other villages.

Social services delivery such as water are being improved in tourist attractions. These also benefit the local communities.

4.4.2   *Negative Impacts*

Although this study was basically on the positive impacts of tourism with regard to poverty alleviation, it is also important to recognise that there are negative impacts that are associated with tourism development. These negative impacts are categorised as direct and indirect effects.

4.4.2.1 Direct Negative Impacts

(a) *Environmental Problems*: Much has been said about the environmental impacts of tourism, for example, pollution, coral reef damage or spoiling the beauty of a palm-fringed beach. Larsen (1998), for instance, notes that apart from the positive impacts from tourism, there are negative environmental impacts, which need to be assessed and addressed properly. ODI (1999) also points out that with increased tourist activities many people suffer reduced access to natural resources and/or degradation of natural resources on which they depend.

(b) *Cultural pollution*: Cultural pollution has been cited as common especially in small island states. In Zanzibar, for example, despite an official preference for low-volume, high-cost tourists, the practice has been to attract back-packers reportedly to have a high (but unspecified) cultural impact on the local Muslim society (Briguglio et al 1996). It is estimated that 95 percent of the population of Zanzibar is Muslim. Therefore the large influx of tourists, most of them being non-Moslem, poses a real danger to the local culture. The situation is further complicated by wide cultural gaps between guest and host. However, studies from Asian countries indicate that fears of tourism threatening local cultures are often misplaced. The cultural changes that accompany tourism are part of the general changes that take place as communities adapt to new economic realities. Some communities are more able to resist the pressure for cultural change (Shah and Gupta, 2000).

(c) *Immoral Behaviour*: There is a type of tourist group commonly known as "hippies' in many of the developing countries. These are mostly young people from the affluent societies who explore the third world in an unstructured manner, trying to identify with the local stream of life. In many of the receiving countries such type of tourists have been associated with immoral behaviours like drug abuse, sexual immorality, loose hygienic standards, crime, laziness and exploitation (O'Grady 1982). It is further noted in ODI (1999), that potentially local cultures and morals are corrupted by contact between the local poor and wealthy hedonist tourist visitors. In particular, tourism tends to encourage prostitution or sex industry. This problem is also noted by Kulindwa, et al (2001), who point out that tourism development creates a fertile ground from which social and cultural problems spring up. The occurring anti-social behaviour and socially unacceptable tendencies include prostitution, drug abuse, alcoholism, child labour and truancy.

4.4.2.2 Indirect Negative Impacts

(a) Exclusion of local people from access to resources: Generally there has been a tendency of excluding local people from land allocated to investors. Although this is not intentional, the practice has been so. This was found to be prominent in Kiwengwa (North Unguja) where some investors have direct exclusive use of near-shore coral reefs, whereas the locals have been denied this right.

(b) Intensified utilization of resources outside tourism areas: The exclusion

of local people from land allocated to tourism investors and the alienation of some resources (such as coral reefs) for tourist purposes has intensified the use of similar resources elsewhere, that is, outside tourism areas.

(c) *Increased utilization of fish and other coastal marine products*: Presence of tourist hotels normally increases the price fishermen receive for their fish and other marine products. But on the other hand, there are no prospects for sustainable supply of these resources as hotel demand could exhaust them. There were reported cases of periodic shortages of some preferred species of fish in hotels in North Unguja (Kiwengwa) and Bagamoyo. However, one has to note that shortages may be a reflection of either exhaustion of resource or limited capacity to fish to meet growing demand.

(d) *Displacement of People from Land*: Local people are displaced from land allocated to hotel developers. There were reported cases of displaced fishermen and seaweed farmers by hotel developers in Kiwengwa. Also, the dominance of employees from outside the local area during hotel construction, partly, reflects the inclusion aspect. Nevertheless, there were no reported cases of conflicts in the study areas resulting from exclusion and inclusion.

4.4.3 *Linkages With the local Economy*

Further analysis was done with respect to linkages between tourism and other sectors of the Tanzanian economy. The Tanzania 1992 Input-Output Table was compressed into 10 by 10 Sectors and estimates were made for Tourism Sector (Table 11).

Table 11: Linkages of Tourism and other Sectors *(Figures in Million Tshs)*

Sector	1	2	3	4	5	6	7	8	9	10	Total
Agriculture	59,102	72	250,902		4,063	23,022	23,022			3,874	341,743
Mining	248	365	4,842		4,394				2,300		12,149
Manufacturing	41,059	991	77,107	1,813	33,843	27,003	34,447	6,308	2,311	22,005	221,778
Electricity & Water	2,259	900	25,023	2,362	575	3,85	21,936	1,126	869	3,478	40,444
Construction	513	102	8,239	674	6,549	1,216	51,766	874	3,052	2,371	74,953
Wholesale, Trade	23,545	354	29,734	2,600	6,296	10,768	5,433	9,062	4,303	28,661	115,321
Tourism	42					40,609		21,109	384	3,565	65,709
Transport/ Communication	7,874	258	6,071	1,678	4,360	26,479	5,258	8,450	3,497	22,697	84,710
Finance	1,297	475	4,433	1,249	2,099	8,883	2,900	5,722	63,169	6,885	95,167
Public Admin	80		2,198	476	540	8,039	765	3,868	3,437	56,749	75,385
Total	139,339	3,619	410,721	11,475	65,747	119,833	127,607	44,722	86,898	179,296	1,127,360

Source: 1992 Input-Output Table for Tanzania.

The linkage between tourism sector as a consumer from other sectors is shown in column seven. In this column it is shown that in terms of input consumption, the three largest supplying sectors were construction, manufacturing and agriculture. However, tourism as a producer and therefore a supplier of inputs to other sectors as shown in row seven, it is observed that the leading recipients were wholesale, retail trade, hotels and restaurants; transport and communication and public administration. Generally, Tourism Sector has high forward and backward linkages.

The linkage between tourism and other sectors was also examined through the sourcing of commodities by hotels in the surveyed areas (See Table 12).

Table 12: Sources of Commodities for Hotels by Sector and Origin, 2001 (Responses of Hotels)

Supplying Sector	Area of Origin						Total		Village
	Within village		Elsewhere in Tanzania		Imports		Total supply for each sector		% of sector from village
(1)	(2)		(3)		(4)		(5)=(2)+(3)+(4)		(2)/(5)
	No.	%	No.	%	No.	%	No.	%	
Fishing	20	12.7	10	5.6	3	3.4	33	7.8	60.6
Farming	62	39.5	59	33.1	13	14.8	134	31.7	46.3
Livestock	54	34.4	27	15.2	5	5.7	86	20.3	62.8
Manufacture		138.3	78	43.8	67	76.1	158	37.4	8.2
Forestry	8	5.1	4	2.3	0	0.0	12	2.8	66.7
Total	157	100.0	178	100.0	88	100.0	423	100.0	37.1

Source: Survey Data, 2001/2002.

Overall, it is observed that within the economy, tourism has high backward linkages in farming and livestock sectors. Out of 134 responses obtaining their commodities from farming (agriculture), 62 of them (46.3 percent) sourced these commodities from within/nearby village. In the livestock, out of 85 responses, 54 of them (63.5 percent) sourced their commodities from within/ nearby village. Commodities of the manufacturing nature are mostly sourced from elsewhere in Tanzania Mainland and imports. But generally, tourism sector appears to have significant linkage with the local economy as the sector-wise contribution of commodities is high in most sectors (except manufacturing) with an overall contribution of 37.1 percent from within the village. This percentage increases to 79.2 percent if sourcing from elsewhere Tanzania Mainland/Zanzibar is included.

5.0   FACTORS INFLUENCING PARTICIPATION

5.1 PARTICIPATION IN TOURIST ACTIVITIES

Participation in tourist related activities by members of households is motivated by, among others things, the expected benefits (employment, incomes), creation of external links and the desire to use the incomes received from tourist related activities to acquire other assets and improve the living standards (See Table 13). Almost all the factors influencing participation in tourism activities have a direct bearing on poverty alleviation.

Table 13: Main Benefits from Tourism Activities in the Surveyed Areas (Responses)

Benefits	Arusha	Bagamoyo	North B	Total	Rank
Income	34	80	48	162	1
A quire other assets (e.g. House)	14	1	4	19	5
Communication/External Links	18	8	1	27	3
Gain experience/skills	4	1	0	5	6
Increase employment opportunities	6	3	26	35	2
Accessibility to social services	13	0	10	23	4
Total	89	93	89	271	

Source: Survey Data, 2001/2002.

5.2 NON-PARTICIPATION IN TOURIST ACTIVITIES

In spite of the potentials for poverty alleviation through participation in tourist activities, not all households or individuals participated in such initiatives. Overall, distance to tourist centres appeared to be a cause for non-participation in tourist activities for the majority of non-participating households. Of the total 65 non-participating households (total coverage 281), 47 households (72.3 percent) were those approaching the 5 kilometres distance. However, apart from the distance issue a number of problems hindering effective participation in tourism activities were identified. Using first mention as the most serious problem affecting the respondent, eight such problems were recorded in the survey areas (Table 14). These problems have been reducing participation in tourist activities. Specifically, the problem of lack of customers ranked first followed by competition and insecurity.

Table 14: Main Problems Hindering Effective Participation in Tourism Activities in the Surveyed Areas

Problems	Arusha	Bagamoyo	North B	Total	Rank
Insecurity/Theft	7	13	11	31	3
Language problem	2	7	0	9	7
Transport/Communication	10	12	1	23	5
Lack of customers	30	42	9	81	1
Competition	19	8	25	52	2
Lack of capital	7	6	0	13	6
Seasonality of business	11	5	8	24	4
Culture distortion	0	0	6	6	8
Total	86	93	60	239	

Source: Survey Data, 2001/2002.

6.0 PERCEPTIONS AND VIEWS ABOUT TOURISM

The discussions above indicate that tourism is indeed one of the important economic activities in the surveyed areas. One purpose of the household survey was to try to assess their perceptions towards tourism. Households' perceptions may provide an important input towards policy formulation process in which consensus on future direction for tourism development is to be directed. Local attitudes and receptiveness to tourists and the sector itself are important issues to be considered. The interviewees were therefore asked to provide their perceptions on how they viewed tourism in relation to other activities. The results on householdsí perception are presented in Figure 8.

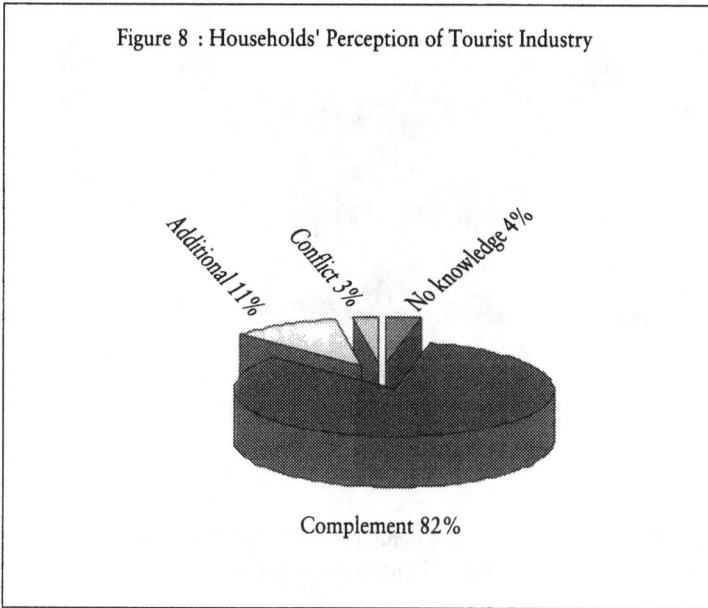

Figure 8 : Households' Perception of Tourist Industry

Additional 11%   Conflict 3%   No knowledge 4%

Complement 82%

Source: Survey Data, 2001/2002.

In general, the information presented in Figure 8 reveals that tourism is regarded as a very important economic activity, which is complementing rather than conflicting other economic activities in the areas of study. 82 percent of the households indicated that tourism related activities were complementing other economic activities.

Further analysis on perception about tourism was done on sectoral basis. Respondents within a given sector were asked how they perceived tourism compared to the sector they were engaged. A summary of the responses is shown in Figure 9.

Figure 9: How Tourism Supports/Conflicts Other Livelihood Activities

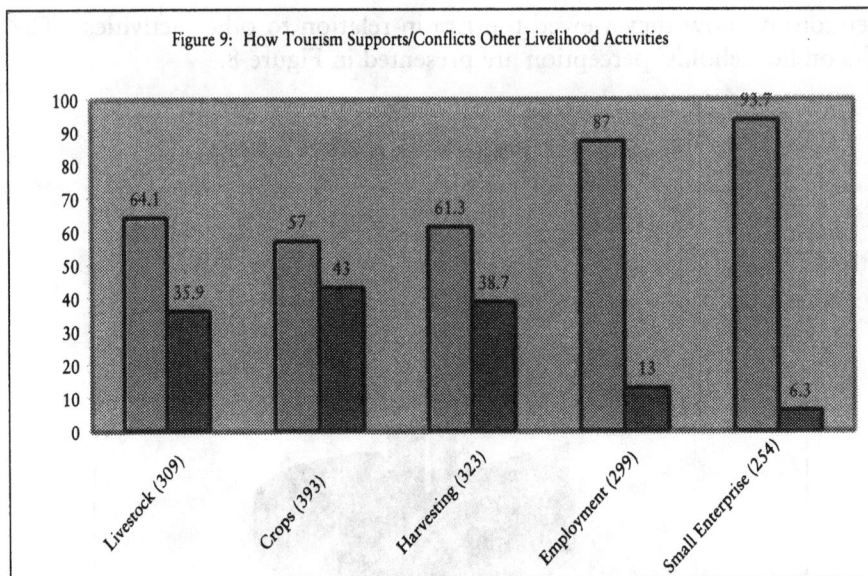

Key: In each livelihood activity, the first column bar represents responses for supporting and the second bar for conflicting. Numbers in parentheses are the total responses in each activity.

Source: Survey Data, 2001/2002.

In all sectors/activities (livestock keeping, crop farming, harvesting, employment and small enterprise), the majority of respondents indicated that tourism was supporting other livelihood activities rather than conflicting with them.

7.0   SUMMARY AND CONCLUSIONS

7.1 SUMMARY

This study investigated the role of tourism in poverty alleviation in three tourist areas of Tanzania (two in the Mainland and one in Zanzibar Isles) with a rural setting. At least two villages/wards were studied in each area. In Arusha Region the studied villages were Mto wa Mbu Barabarani in Monduli District and Kilimamoja in Karatu District. In Coast Region two wards, namely Magomeni and Dunda were studied in Bagamoyo town. And in North Unguja Region in Zanzibar the studided villages were Kiwengwa-Cairo, Kiwengwa-Gulioni and

Kiwengwa Kumbaurembo all located in North B district. All these areas have a total of 6,816 households out of which 281 or about 4.1 percent of the responding households provided adequate information that was utilized in this study.

Several economic activities are practiced in the areas of study with varying degrees. Generally, tourist related economic activities are commonly practiced in all three areas of the study. However, taking into account that all areas are of a rural setting, there is also significant participation in agricultural sector (both farming and livestock). Thus apart from sale/provision of tourist related products such as tour operation, curio shops and handcraft, supply and sale of agricultural products are also important. However, there are differences in the intensity/importance of participation in the different economic activities amongst the three areas of study.

The main objective of this study was to analyse the direct and indirect livelihood impacts from tourism and their implications for poverty alleviation. The sector being the fastest growing sector in Tanzania, the study intended to investigate the benefits and costs of tourism on the society in general and on the poor in particular. In order to achieve this objective the study dwelt on questions related to generation of foreign exchange and public revenues, employment, incomes, accessibility to assets and basic needs and their effects on the poor, and the linkages of tourism to the local economy. Both positive and negative aspects were studied. Issues affecting participation/non-participation in tourism and the way respondents perceived tourism were examined.

Both qualitative and quantitative information collected was subsequently used in the analysis. Using the results, the study has established that:

(a) Tourism contributes significantly to the national economy through employment generation, foreign exchange earnings and public revenues. However, the sector is sensitive/delicate to global instability caused by phenomena such as terrorism and/or war.

(b) Tourism is an important economic activity in the areas of study particularly in activities such as tour operation, curio shops and handcraft sales. However, agricultural activities are also practised.

(c) Tourism is significant on both direct and indirect employment opportunities. Directly, it is observed that there was substantial employment generation in hotels as out of a total 1,114 employees, 1,056 (95 percent) were Tanzanians. But these employment opportunities for the locals were mainly observed to be in the lower cadres with low educational/skills requirements and low pay. Indirectly, there was significant local participation in tourist related activities where 346 people or 50.7 percent of the economically active residents (683) in the three areas of the study indicated that they were participating in such activities[14]. Both males (277 people or 80 percent) and females (69 people or 20 percent) were participating.

(d) There is no observable general pattern of increasing contribution of incomes from tourism to households. But there is a general increase in the number of people receiving incomes from tourist related activities. Given the fact or the 'common norm' that always it is difficult to get income data from individuals/households, the increase in number may be interpreted as a reflection of increasing opportunities for getting incomes from tourist activities. Moreover, the results reveal significant direct and indirect employment opportunities. Those opportunities provide important sources of incomes to the households.

(e) Cultural tourism is emerging as an important tourist activity especially in Arusha and Bagamoyo. Given that this type of activity does not require specialised skills and the incomes accrues directly to the performer, it should be viewed positively as a way of reducing poverty in rural areas.

(f) Locals perceive tourism to be important and that it generally complements and supports rather than conflicting other economic activities. About 82 percent of those interviewed perceived tourism to be complementing as opposed to only 3 percent who thought that tourism was conflicting other economic activities.

(g) Tourism contributes substantially to increased asset ownership and basic needs or livelihoods requirements of the households. However, at times there are competitions or conflicts in the use of resources between tourist activities and other/social economic activities.

(h) Tourism has strong linkages to other sectors both at national level and at local areas of the study. It has strong backward linkages to sectors and activities that most poor people participate in. The linkages thus create opportunities for locals to benefit and alleviate poverty.

---

[14] Total number of participation in various activities was 1050 from which 367 was deducted to account for the young, students and inactive.

(i) There are some unquantifiable negative impacts of tourism that may act against the positive impact on poverty alleviation. These include, among other things, loss of access to resources, environmental degradation, distortion of traditional culture and immoral behaviour.

Overall, tourism development has shown to play an important role towards poverty alleviation. Tourism has the potential to have both forward and backward linkages to become a pro-poor growth sector. However, there are times when tourism development competes with other activities (normally more familiar to local people) in the use of resources available. Competition may result in the diminishing of resources such as land, water, wood and marine products. Depending on the magnitude of the dependency on these resources, the quality of life may as well be affected in the same way (most probably negatively) as the pressure on those resources increase.

There are also some negative impacts that need to be dealt with for sustenance of the positive impacts. The study has, therefore, also established why some households are not participating in tourism and hence being less successful in alleviating their poverty. Thus, policies directed at solving the constraints, which inhibit people from participating in tourism were looked at for the purpose of proposing how participation could be enhanced.

7.2 Policy Implications

This study examined how participation in tourism activities can contribute towards poverty alleviation in a sustainable manner. Generally, the results from this study indicate that tourism has high potential for poverty alleviation. However, there are policy issues that need to be addressed for the sector's effective contribution towards that goal. Such issues, among other things, include the following:

(a) Tourism and its related activities should be promoted not only in the areas of study, but also in other parts of the country with tourist attractions.

(b) The fragile nature of tourism sector puts into test the stability on the standard of living on those dependent on it. It is therefore of crucial importance to encourage participants in the tourism sector both at national and local levels to diversify their investment portfolios. Thus for sustainability of poverty alleviation strategies, diversification of sources for the livelihood requirements need to be encouraged. Additionally, promotion of domestic tourism need to be encouraged.

(c) Employment opportunities for the locals are observed to be in the low cadres with low skills and remuneration. In order to increase the impact of tourism on poverty alleviation, there is need to institute training programmes that would ultimately provide chance for the locals to be employed in high cadres with high pay.

(d) Cultural tourism is emerging as an important tourist attraction with no significant investment requirements. Given that in most parts of rural Tanzania the majority have low education and lack of capital, this type of tourism need to be encouraged in order to contribute towards poverty alleviation.

(e) Generally, tourism is highly import dependent and therefore with substantial impact on the balance of payments. To minimize the negative impacts on the balance of payments, there is need to enhance the linkage of tourism sector to the local economy.

(f) The negative impacts such as environmental problems, cultural pollution and immoral behaviour, which are a cost and hence reducing the positive impacts, or benefits from tourism must be dealt with. Thus, whereas there is need to optimise the benefits from tourism, measures and policies to minimize cultural pollution, environmental conservation and protection need to be promoted and supported in tourist areas for sustainable development.

7.3 EXPECTED BENEFITS FROM THE STUDY AND DISSEMINATION OF THE RESULTS

This study is expected to be useful to policy makers in terms of the above mentioned policy implications. It will also help other participants and non-participants in tourism related activities. Academicians will also benefit from the additional literature of the study itself.

Dissemination of the results is expected to be made through REPOA Seminar/ Workshop and REPOA Publication.

7.4 FUTURE RESEARCH WORK

Future research work arising from this study could possibly examine the following issues:

(a) An application of more quantitative methods to analyse the economic impact of tourism.

(b) Investigate the magnitude of leakages from tourism so as to find out how these can be minimized in order that a country and local participants could increase their earnings from tourism and subsequently alleviate poverty.

(c) Study of size and implications employment and income multipliers in tourism.

(d) Study of potential and avenues for economic diversification in areas of this study.

(e) Promotion of domestic tourism.

REFERENCES

Andronicou, A. (1979). 'Tourism in Cyprus', in de Kadt (eds.) *Tourism - Passport to Development?*, Oxford University Press.

Ashley, C. (2000). "The Impact of Tourism on Rural Livelihoods: Namibia's Experience", London: Overseas Development Institute (ODI) Paper 128.

_____ et al (2000). "Pro-Poor Tourism: Putting Poverty at the Heart of the Tourism Agenda", ODI Paper Number 51.

Benavides, D. (2001). "Is the socio-economic sustainability of International Tourism assured under hyper-competitive conditions?" *www.sommets-tourisme.org*

Bird, R. M. (1992). 'Taxing Tourism in Developing Countries', *World Development*, Vol. 20, No. 8, pp. 1145-1158.

BoT (1999). *Economic and Operations Report,* Dar es Salaam: Bank of Tanzania, (June).

Briguglio, L et al (eds.) (1996). *Sustainable Tourism in Island and Small States: Case Studies.* London and New York: Acassell Imprint.

Bryden, J.M. (1973). *Tourism and Development: A Case Study of the Commonwealth Caribbean*; Cambridge: Cambridge University Press.

Chachage, L. (1998). 'Adjustment, Globalization and Transformation in Mining and Tourism in Tanzania', paper prepared for conference on Structural Adjustment and Socio-Economic Change in Sub-Saharan Africa, Organized by the Nordic Africa Institute, Copenhagen, (3-5, December).

Carney, D. (ed) (1998), *Sustainable Rural Livelihoods: What Contributions can we make*, London:n.p.

Cukier, J. Norris, J and Wall G. (1996). 'The Involvement of Women in the Tourism Industry of Bali, Indonesia', *The Journal of Development Studies,* Vol. 33, No. 2, (December), pp. 248-270.

De Kadt, E (eds.) (1979). *Tourism - Passport to Development?* Oxford University Press.

Dieke, P. U. C. (1993). 'Tourism in The Gambia: Some Issues in Development Policy', *World Development,* Vol. 21, No. 2, pp.277-89.

Focus Multimedia (1997). Tourism: Focus on Tunisia. *www.focusmm.com.*

Gee, C. Y. (eds.) (1997). *International Tourism: A Global Perspective,* Washington, D.C.: WTO.

Huit, G (1979). 'The Sociocultural Effects of Tourism in Tunisia: A Study of Sousse.' in de Kadt (eds.) op.cit.

Juma M.L., M.H. Ali (1999). 'Tourism development and Change of Life Standards: A Case Study of Two Coastal Villages of Zanzibar'. Mimeo.

Kulindwa and Mashindano (1999). "Macro Economic Reforms and Sustainable Development in Southern Africa. Tanzania Tourism Case Study", Dar es Salaam: Economic Research Bureau (August).

Larsen, K. (1998). *A Case Study on Tourism, Economic Growth and Resource Management in Zanzibar, Tanzania,* Washington, D.C.: The World Bank.

Luvanga, N. and Bol, D. (1999). 'The Impact of Tanzania's Trade and Exchange Regime on Exports', Report for HIID Project on 'Restarting and Sustaining Growth and Development in Tanzania', (November).

_____ (2000). "Tourism Dynamics in Developing Countries: A Review of Evidence", REPOA Research Report.

Maina-wa- Kinyatti (1980). 'Tourism Industry and Development: Kenya Experience', *Philosophy-and-Social-Action,* Vol. 6, No. 1, January-March, pp. 23-31.

Malta Tourism Authority (2001). Tourism: Malta. *www.mta.com.mt*

Mjema G.D., J. Shitundu, T.S. Nyoni (1998). "Tourism as an Export Sector in Tanzania: Literature Survey of the Potential and Problems existing in the sector", paper presented at Economic Research Bureau seminar, 24-3-98, UDSM.

Ndulu B., J. Semboja, A. Mbelle (1998). "Promoting Non-Traditional Exports in Tanzania", paper for UNU/WIDER project.

Noronha, R. (1979), "Paradise Reviewed: Tourism in Bali", in de Kadt (eds.) op.cit.

O'Grady, R. (1982), *Tourism in the Third World: Christian Reflections*, Geneva: World Council of Churches.

Okoso-Amaa, K. (1995), "Marketization of Tourism in Tanzania", Department of Marketing, Occasional Paper Series.

Overseas Development Institute (ODI) (1999). "Sustainable Tourism and Poverty Elimination Study". A Report to the Department for International Development, April.

Shah, K., and Gupta, V. (2000). "Tourism, the poor and other stakeholders: Asian Experience" London: ODI Fair Trade in Tourism paper.

Shivji, I. (1973) (eds.). "Tourism and Socialist Development", *Tanzania Studies*, No. 3, Dar es Salaam: University of Dar es Salaam.

Sinclair, M. T. (1998). 'Tourism and Economic Development: A Survey', *The Journal of Development Studies*, Vol. 34, No. 5, (June).

Sinclair, M. T., Alizadeh Parvin and Elizabeth Atieno Onunga (1995). "The Structure of International Tourism and Tourism Development in Kenya", in D. Harrison (ed.), *Tourism and the Less Developed Countries*. N.p: n.p.

Stynes, D.J. (1999). "Approaches to Estimating the Economic Impacts of Tourism: Some Examples, *home.data.com.ch/econ-turismo/links/impact*, January.

Sulaiman, M. (1996). "Islands within Islands: Exclusive Tourism and Sustainable Utilization of Coastal Resources in Zanzibar". In Briguglio et al (eds).

URT (1999). *The National Tourism Policy*, Dar es Salaam: Ministry of Natural Resources and Tourism, (May).

_____ (1999). *Hali ya Uchumi Kwa Mwaka 1998*. Dar es Salaam: Tume ya Mipango.

_____ (1999). "A Study on Tourism in Tanzania", Dar es Salaam: Ministry of Natural Resources and Tourism. (Draft Report, June)

_____ (2000). *Hali ya Uchumi wa Taifa Katika Mwaka 1999*, Dar es Salaam: Tume ya Mipango.

_____ (2002). *Hali ya Uchumi wa Taifa Katika Mwaka 2001*, Dar es Salaam: Tume ya Mipango.

WTO (1999a), 'Tourism Highlights 1999', (May).

WTO (1999b), 'Compendium of Tourism Statistics 1993-1997', Nineteenth Edition (Madrid).

www.ingramcontent.com/pod-product-compliance
Lightning Source LLC
Chambersburg PA
CBHW061840220326
41599CB00027B/5355